THE REAL REASON

a poetic memoir

MADISSON BEDNARK

The Real Reason: A Poetic Memoir

Published by Snail's Pace Press Ltd.
Highlands Ranch, CO

Copyright © 2024 by Madisson Bednark. All rights reserved.

No part of this book may be reproduced in any form or by any mechanical means, including information storage and retrieval systems without permission in writing from the publisher/author, except by a reviewer who may quote passages in a review.

All images, logos, quotes, and trademarks included in this book are subject to use according to trademark and copyright laws of the United States of America.

ISBN: 979-8-218-40536-6 (paperback)

POETRY / Women Authors

Cover design by Madisson Bednark, copyright owned by Madisson Bednark.
Interior layout by Asya Blue.
Headshot Credit: Taylor Belle Photography

Disclaimer: The conversations in this book all come from the author's recollections. They are not written to represent word-for-word transcripts, but rather to evoke the feelings of the author's experiences.

All rights reserved by Madisson Bednark and Snail's Pace Press Ltd.
Printed in the United States of America.

CONTENTS

•

Revolting Soil 1
Cursed Constellation 3
Rivers Run Through Her 6
Shipwrecked Brick 14
Spellbound 26
Don't Eat Meat 28
Restorative Injustice 38
Narcissist-itis 50
Flower Power 54
You Had Me At Cello 56
Identity Cry-Sis 60
Granular Discomfort 66
No 69
Buried Treasure 70
Scrolling 76
Send Noods 77
A Won Woman Army 82
Erosion 87
We Are Enough 90
5:55 91
Home Is Where the Hospital Is 92
Texture 95
Toujours Chez Moi 99

DEDICATION

•

To my ancestors, who survived so that I could live.

To my loved ones, for believing.

To the parts of me that were brave enough to heal, audacious enough to speak, and delusional enough to believe that truth can change the world.

To you reader, and all the rebel embers who have been stomped on, pissed on, and abandoned, yet continue to burn. May the entire forest feel your flames.

The act of sharing our scars is revolutionary, this is for us.

The Real Reason includes content that
might not be suitable for some readers.

CONTENT WARNINGS

Includes sensitive material relating to: memories of childhood emotional trauma, ableism, racism, death, homophobia, rape/sexual assault, eating disorders, and the justice system in the context of sexual assault.

Revolting Soil

The first stage of trauma is rupture.
The second stage,
        trying to stop the bleeding.
Stop the nightmares.
Power through emotional outages.
Straddle the lines of convergence
Where past and present shake hands.

Navigating nonsense is murky.
So I strangle my internal compass,
To move me in any direction but backward.

Is the third stage acceptance?
No.
I can never accept what's been done.
I refuse to accept violence.

Instead, I think of trauma as a fresh vegetable
        tossed carelessly upon the forest floor.
It sits,
        and rots,
                slowly molding,
Mutating.

Fuzzy fungus overtakes the fruit,
        outwardly appearing as if
                this is the end.
But when viewed back in Time Lapse,
The curtain is pulled back,
Exposing the last true stage of healing.

Decomposition.

The fruit,
Slowly absorbed back into the earth
Repurposed as fuel,
To gas up the next generation.

Without this sacred process of decay,
Earth would quickly overflow with remains.
A decline from gross accumulation,
No new growth,
A famine of fertilization.

These pages are my pain slowly dissolving,
Decomposing back into shared soil.
My story and memory will not be forgotten,
  but transformed.
It will be the food that allows another to grow
  from seedling to tree.
Just as my body will wrinkle and rot,
Turn rancid,
  inciting disgust.
So will my story,
The Real Reason will be used,
To start a revolution:
Resisting the acceptance of violence.

Cursed Constellation

I used to think that I was fragile,
Broken,
Beset with
      misfortune and fury.
Cut open from my throat to my knees,
Organs stolen,
Incinerated without permission.
Sewn back together in a hurry,
Gifted with scars that never heal.
If spilled blood counted as currency,
I could afford
      necessary therapy.

Every few centuries
A star is birthed into a family constellation.
Fortuitous or by design,
Genetic hands are dealt haphazardly.
Like a dusty old recipe,
Pain is passed from generation to generation
Until it's absorbed by a sensitive soul.
Their superpower,
      charged by the electricity of emotions.
Their skeleton,
      a conduit bolted into the ground.
Where pain strikes down,
Demanding to be felt.

My body is burdened by buried sorrows,
Sickened by a generational curse of avoidance.
As fallout,
My soul packed itself up in a Gypsy Caravan,
Brimming with baggage.

A wandering paradox of weird,
Infected by the seriously mysterious.
A poetic oddity,
Collecting strange strains,
Wrought with anxiety,
    disease,
        and battle fatigue.

Sensitive to the touch.
Plagued by idiopathic impurities.
Shameful of the space I take up,
That oftentimes
    I feel too much.
It is my destiny to detoxify a shared sardonic fate,
So I live as a liver
To appease the familial ache.
Accumulating
    and transmuting,
        filtering
    and removing,
An organ built to alleviate waste.

Is this a curse?
Mere misfortune?
I used to think that I was broken,
Until fury released me from the prison of praying.
I no longer beg
    for my sensitivity to go away.
Ancient agony howls within my bones,
Singing a sweet surrender to the celestial current.
My body is but a rock in a river,
A star within a bigger constellation.

Inherited energy drifted through our lineage,
Seeking a worthy healer
        and it found me.
Pain cannot be healed,
If you refuse to feel it.

So I feel.

Rivers Run Through Her

A shimmering veil of displeasure captures
My body with seizure.
This land of mine is scarred
With stripes and pits,
      punctuated with cellulitic divots
            and unmentionable bits.
Singed,
Burnt to the third degree from a ravenous binge.

Whimpers of pain
Whip through cursed corridors.
Carving arches into blushing rock faces,
      etching tattered wrinkles
            into aged formations.

Traversing this type of terrain,
Could warrant a summitting award,
      an explorer's erotic endeavor.
But this wild land is stained with danger,
Collecting lost souls
            and wanderers.
An unholy world that will eat you whole,
Not even the barked ears of trees
      will hear you scream.

This shrine of mine has been defaced,
Vandalized perpetually.
With too many misdeeds to confess,
I repent on the altar of reflection,
Entirely
      undressed.
Mirror, mirror.

There's no fairness in this world at all,
Only candor offered by reflection
And the depravity that warps
      self-image into self-degradation.
I need to be freed,
From this agony of seeing,
From this body that's triggering,
From this landscape that's smoldering.

Eclipsed by the staggering brightness of the sun,
In the starkness of contrast
Is where the depth of my darkness is unshielded,
      revealing beneath
           a rageful dysfunction.
Blanketed by patina,
Synapses rust in the chassis of my mind,
Further fueling dysmorphic ganglia
That outline the curvature of my spine.

Dark rivers run through me,
Flowing with industrial strength inadequacy,
Screaming their way
Through my blackened silt soils.
Soils, long since stripped of fecundity
      for the sake of vanity.

My present reality
      gifts cramps of agony.
Not because of a putrid poison I ate,
But because,
      I lack the willpower to self-regulate.

To purge is to be rid of,
To expel the darkness that's buried
      beneath freckled skin,

To scour compulsory sins,
To annul devious weakness.

As the dictator,
And inhabitant of this dysphoric land,
I am both the punished,
      and the punisher.

Fertilized by one last steadfast bite,
My stomach shutters in volatile spasms,
      disgorging a ground-shaking growl.
A subterranean detonation of sound
Is sent deep underground,
With a roaring ripple, alerting my last lifeline
To take flight.
In an acute exodus,
My coal canary flies its perch
      having sensed an excess of foreign substance.
An odorless,
      colorless,
           gas
Begins to emerge,
Visceral walls crumble and cave,
      forcibly giving way.
The shafts of my mind collapse.

I can no longer endure the torture of
My clothes and the skin I'm in,
      fitting agonizingly tight.
Just as in nature,
      wildfires are required.
Self-controlled cropping is what
I desperately desire.

I must trim the fat,
        prune the pounds,
                burn it all to the ground.

A rancid belch betrays me,
Something putrid has infiltrated
The lining of my intestine.
An intense heat,
Growls from yeasted guilt,
        blooming within.

The interstitial ocean between my organs
Writhes with a grudgeful tide.

My mind,
        a medieval apothecary.
Willing to administer strange sadistic medicine,
In the hope that it will
        cure me.
In the hope that it won't
        kill me.

The only way to lose weight at this rate,
Is to spew the subdermal crude oil that's
        been churning,
                bubbling,
                        rotting.
So I trace the mountainous landscape of my lips,
Watch in amazement
        as the sun sets behind my eyes.

Ushering in adventure,
        a plunge to the depths.
I find myself immersed in the one thing
I truly despise,
                me.

With my mouth open wide,
Along its articulated fault,
Two fingers of choice palpate the back
    of my throat.
With their intuition as a bewitched guide,
They know precisely what to do,
How much pressure to apply.
How much dynamite is needed to power
    a synchronous coup.

My middle and index stage a rebellious gag reflex.

These weapons of mass destruction,
Have become my weapons
    of mass reduction.
Generating seismic waves aimed
    at my epicenter.
Where buried wrongdoings begin throbbing,
As this natural disaster
Slithers upwards from my core
    with an impending eruption.

Heaving and lurching,
    untamed and wild.
My hair gets pulled back
Into a one-handed bunker,
Each strand preparing for impact.
Even the tears welling up inside my aqueducts,
    pause
        retreat
            and take cover.

Magmic bile climbs up my esophagus,
Surging past teeth with a bedabbling

Splash.
It gurgles for a moment then sinks to the bottom
    of bleached palatial porcelain.
From a praying position,
    my head levitates.
Emerging with an acid-soaked grin,
Accented with a shameful
    saliva bearded chin.

I can still hear that splash,
    even all these years later,
It's ingrained like a mosquito in the soul
    of my ambered sap.
Eating disorders are a malaria of the mind,
An inhumane bated trap.

No inoculation could've prevented the war waged
On my young body.
On the mental health
    of my young self.
Am I hungry?
A cookie?
I couldn't possibly.
Perhaps a piece of gum?
Only once I've settled my debts with diuretics
    emptying all that's left.
Sentences sputter on empty,
Joyously numb.
Hunger.
I am hungry to be skinny.
Promised that life will be better,
I'll be happier,
    and prettier,
        people will like me more.
I'll be adored.

It matters not if I feel full,
As long as people think I'm beautiful.

American girl.

Little fingers skim the surface of social media,
Idolizing fake flesh,
Shrinking skin to fit expectations.
Sick.
Drugged with Ozempic.
Dressing up in mommy's heels
And daddy's fatphobic rhetoric.

Beauty standards are
Beauty failures.

They are failing us,
They are killing us.

Succumbing to the herbicidal poison,
We weed ourselves out.
Therefore contributing to a generational curse
      of forfeiting our rights.
Rights to exist equally in a world that's diverse.
A box of beauty has become our sanatorium,
Where we go to lose ourselves
      in its madness.
This is where they lobotomize our humanness.
Bleach, what makes us each unique
      and exorcize our fatness.

I think back to the moment of conception,
When this poison inside of me
      was first consumed.

I can trace it all back to the first deception.
The moment I lied to myself,
Proclaiming weight loss
        as a self-love prescription.

The moment I believed what my dad said.

The moment I tied my value to my waist.

The moment diet culture ate my safe space.

For decades I set fire to my wild,
        blinded and beguiled,
Not a single tributary of truth
        was in sight.

Today, dark rivers still run through me,
But on this side of the sickness affliction
        alpenglow paints pink horizons of hope.

My eyes wait patiently at the edge of truth,
Believing for the first time
        that even a hesitant sun
                will eventually rise.

This land of mine is sacred.
And the only substance worth purging
Is lies.

Shipwrecked Brick

My house,
        bricked and blue
Harbored in a gray suburban ocean
Afloat,
        but just barely.
The steel hulled barge is riddled
        with holes of resentment,
Each one punctured by sharp fanged secrets,
Ship sinking secrets.
So salaciously salty,
Packing enough salinity to brine every pickle
        in Manhattan and Brooklyn deli.
The greatest secret unbeknownst to all
        is that this bricked,
                two story house
                        that's painted blue,
Is swiftly sinking and splintering into   two.

We've been sideswiped.
Each wrought iron rivet splits in half,
Exposing cylindrical rust ridden shafts.
The pressure,
        ratcheting.
Emotions,
        mounting.

Internal alarms, triggered in succession
From injurious shaking.
Each hair sewn into my arm pulls like thread,
        snagged,
                standing on end.

Walls begin to lose form,
Folding in along their creases.
Each second that passes
Fills starboard compartments with water so cold,
The dust on our comforters freezes.

Everything's coming undone.
I am but a child,
Not the carpenter of this ship,
      or the reason for this dynasty's demise.
From the moment we set sail,
      sickness set in.
Internal squelching demanded a summoning
      of seaworthy legs,
And a fattening of thicker blubber skin.
A toughened hide
      tanned to withstand
            the tough love given.

My tragic truth of Titanic proportions
Is that no amount of preparedness
Would save me from this mess.
From being the youngest,
      the outlier,
            the odd girl out.
Each lifeboat already at capacity,
Toting seven siblings,
      all bonded by blood.
They huddle together to survive for another hour.
But when I look down around my chest,
I see no vestige of preservation,
      no flotation contraption,
           no life vest.
So here I cower,
Perched up a withered mast, screaming a warning.

Prophetic messages, obtusely ignored,
Bottled up,
    corked,
        and washed up ashore.

I sprint to the deck,
To grab a glimpse of the iceberg
That's so brazenly robbed our last
    stitch of sanctity.
Alas,
There's no ice in sight.
I see what's under the sea.
A deep-water Kraken lurking in the brew beneath.
It's waiting for us to self-destruct,
    for our familial empire to fall.
Inky black eyes track back and forth eagerly,
Counting down the minutes
    left on the pressure cooker timer.
Its mythos,
    is as grand as its hunger.

Silently wading.

Expertly angling with tentacles of superstition.
This monster intends to fulfill its foretold forecast
As chronicled by stupefied seamen,
To swallow us whole.

What can you expect
When two families are cut and pasted together?
Forcibly recruited
    and dragooned.
Affixed like wet tissue paper
To a phoenix's feather,
A fantasy.

Two previously combusted families
        cannot resurrect anew.

It's unrealistic to think
That staples and glue, slathered on thick,
Prayers from the non-ecclesiastic,
Hollow threats and daggered coercion,
Can make us stick.

I am told this will work,
        told this will hold,
If only we persevere.
But each breath I expel feels as though it will be
        my last.
Suffocating slowly,
Anoxic
        from
                fear.

In the same breath that he exclaims
I suck at math
        and I'm no good at singing,
He belts out that I'm too sensitive,
        and maybe that's true.
I'm sensitive enough
        to sense that this yelling is killing us.
Alarms fill the air as CO_2 builds in the room,
He's stoking the fire,
And closed the flue.

Fear is changing us.
It's simultaneously sharpening our knives
        and shortening our lives.
It's softening us.

The dinner table is set with a malignant spread.
Let's all dig in.
My brothers say grace by berating us to our faces.
Calling us
    slut,
        bitch,
            cunts.
Who will throw the first punch?
Will the cops get called?
Who's ready for seconds?

Dessert is a small wooden lance,
    sharpened at both ends,
        used to pick deceit from our teeth.

Our teeth
    are falling out.
Is it scurvy?
A deficiency of vitamin C?
    or more likely,
It's the rotten words that we feed to each other.
The putrid hate we regurgitate,
    exchanged with non-consensual mouths.
It's eating us alive with an eternal hunger,
    no amount of family therapy
        can satiate this disease.

The blue bricked house,
    is now a battleship.
Painted for war.
Haunted by soulless soldiers.
Strung out on pills, coke, and alcohol.
Mood swings seesaw
    from suicidal to homicidal.

I lock my door,
        to keep them from stealing,
                to thwart their thieving disorder.
These are not siblings, their only true family is crime.
The drugs they peddle
Attract scumbags with machetes,
        concealed in their baggy jeans.

Rich in overdoses,
        a common occurrence.
Their dad,
        common sense poor.
He ignores red flags,
So our possessions are traded for dime bags,
How can I feel safe anymore?

At bedtime,
        when I whisper my prayers
I ask,
Lay me down to sleep in the trenches of the deep,
Cold and comatose,
Is the peace that I seek.

Angels,
        I pray,
That as I slip into slumber,
That my soul doesn't drift too deep
        into the forgotten,
Too deep to be retrieved.

When the angels don't answer, I ask my mother.

"Why Mommy?
Why am I not allowed
        to make a sound?"

"My darling for they feed on fear.
You can pray
        but my love,
If you are weak, you will be the prey.
Things will get better,
        so do what I say.
Our Captain knows best, stay the course."

Stranded in the darkest corner of my bedroom,
I cry until I vomit.
Snotting and choking,
With a laborious cough
        a few sparse words make their escape.
Bobbing up,
        to my sensitive surface,
                with great haste.
I say,
"It's no secret.
Everyone here hates each other."
I beg to run away.

My voice of reason responds,
"Stop
        stop
                stop crying!
Choke on your tears like pills,
        perhaps as a prophylactic
                for your dramatic."

So I stop.
Stop crying,
        stop choking,
                stop hoping.

The incessant rocking of ebb and flow,
I languish that this is the life I have,
But it's the life
        I never chose.

Drunk from nausea,
I fall to the floor.
Dropping my ear to the bottom of the door.
Finding the pinprick
        of light that seeps through,
Honing in on the sound that carries
Like steadfast ashen pigeons.

My ear,
She's my auricle of intuition,
        and this,
This is the only place where I get my answers,
To hear firsthand
        if indeed
                I am the pressure system
                      that caused this storm.

Wondering to myself,
        what did I do this time?

They scream back and forth, blaming each other.
Hating how the other one
        parents their daughter.
I smother my breath, so my peeping isn't discovered.
It's no secret,
        but I wish they knew.
This bricked blue ship has finally cracked into two.

As I lay caught in the current of this
        midnight hurricane,

I surrender to its abuse.
It guzzles me whole, with a wrathful whitewash.
Black tainted water
      forcibly breathed into my diseased lungs,
Wheezed into my bloodstream,
Until I can't take in anymore.
I am unable to decipher if the sound I hear
      is my heart beating,
Or, if it's the scream of my soul
Knocking on death's door.

In an instant,
This sound is transformed
      into shrewd silence.

My eardrums rupture.
The aqueous humor behind my eyes overflows
      and floods,
It runs red,
      and turns to blood.

My body is decimated.
But there's an ease of stillness
      to being suffocated.

Am I sedated, or asleep?
Am I even alive?

When morning comes,
I hazily open my eyes.
Admittedly, they are encrusted with surprise.
I guess the Kraken showed mercy on me,
      because I survived.

All that's left are broken bottles with sandy messages,
Drunkenly scribbled in each other's blood.
I look down to my arm,
It's crimson and cut,
The letters were written with
      the ink of self-harm.

These lacerations need stitches,
But to my dismay,
There's nobody left to provide me aid.
The ship's been abandoned,
      all except for one.
I reckon they had to cut their losses,
Perhaps I couldn't be saved.

So here I lay,
      dehydrating in the sun.
Holding the blue bricks from our beloved ship.
Clutching them, with newfound adoration,
      we are the only wreckage that's left.
They quickly slip from my fingertips,
Dripping down
      to the whiskey doused ground,
Becoming one with the mud.

The thing about mud,
Besides being sloppy and unsavory,
It's the cement that seals our eternal tombs.
Enveloping us when we're laid to rest,
Uniting us all,
      in the graveyard
            of our mother's womb.

This is where it all starts,
And where it all ends.

On the rocky shores,
Where we shiver in the frigid sea spray
    and daggered quicksand,
On the foreboding cliffs edge,
Where we resist the jump.

Childhood trauma is the mud we're all left with,
When we've survived the sheer cliffs
    and wrecked ships.
It's the real reason wiry gray color
Storms through haggard hair.
It's sealed in the mantle of our pores,
Volcanically erupting as sebaceous cystic acne.
Polka-dotted topically,
Resurfacing the entirety of our bodies.

It's in us,
    it covers us,
        it breaks us,
            it makes us.

You cannot simply wash it from you.
So we've been taught to transform our mud
    into masks,
To conform.
Our armor must be painted and decorated aesthetically.
Society can't fathom seeing our trauma so plainly,
So undisguised.
People are intimidated by the naked,
For it reflects their pain,
Reminders of their own shipwreck
    when the sun didn't rise.
The nights cloaked in darkness, when they walked alone.
It reminds them of the ghosts
That haunt their own home.

Not me.

I welcome the sight of exposed muddied masks.
Those that are cracked,
Unpainted by performative positivity.
The raw faces of the brave.
I see beauty in wearing trauma plainly,
Knowing it didn't bury you
In an untimely grave.

Here you stand,
ON
The ground
      and not
            IN.
You survived the greatest battle of all,
The one with your kin.

Spellbound

I don't have a daughter,
But sometimes I daydream
About the fairy-tale hues that I would use
To paint her a picture of possibility.

Knowing that her ears will hear many stories,
About the constraints of womanhood,
Fables of her fragility,
Casting spells of doubt,
      about her abilities,
Limiting the expanse of the greatness she sees.
What parable can weigh more than these words?
What enchantment can I plant in her mind's eye
      that will make her believe
           in her magic?

My words are enough,
      and so is she,
So I say to her heart,
That it's big and bold;
Beating strongly, she's perfectly capable.
Her soul paints in broad strokes of bravery,
She is much more than just her beauty.
No matter what forces she faces,
Not even the claustrophobic panic
      of a glass ceiling
           can contain her,
Only her own limiting beliefs.

I place my faith in her daring spirit,
Knowing that it will steer her feet upwards

To mountaintops,
      boardrooms,
           the outer reaches of space.

I don't have a daughter,
But I am a daughter,
      an apprentice under a master.
My mother raised me to say these words to myself
      on the days that I struggle to exist
           in this nonsensical world.
A world that tries to brick us into the confines of castles,
Handcuffing us in shackles.
We do not exist to be saved,
Our stories are written
By the pen
      of our independence.
All daughters are limitless.

Words are spells, ignited by intention,
      when ingested they act as a potion.
Sipping self-love, conjures conviction.
But when bewitched by critique, we bleed.
When I hear doubt creep into my mind,
      I know it's a man's voice
           and not mine.
So I speak to myself with kindness,
To be the kind of parent I need.

Don't Eat Meat

The real reason I'm vegan
        is because I know what it's like
                to be eaten.

To be hunted,
To be tortured,
To be used for your "meat."
Skinned alive by violent men,
        hung by your feet.
Suspended in a tree like a strand of
Cheap Christmas lights,
        twinkling with fear.

Only seconds to ruminate
On the entirety of your life,
And
To calculate the probability
That you'll bleed out
        on their knife.

How can fault be assigned to me
        for looking so appetizing?
I didn't see that my life was in danger.
My vision, hindered by the
        buxom bounce of my teenage cheeks.

My juvenile denial,
Cloaking an unseen hunting ground
        behind a camouflaged veil.
I couldn't comprehend the allure
Of my prepubescent mystique.

I am guilty,
But only
       of traipsing into sordid cross hairs.
What horrifically happened after that,
I couldn't possibly prevent.

It was undoubtedly him,
Dressed in an orange vest that sealed my fate.
His stomach,
       hungering for me.
Taste buds,
Perceiving me as mouth-wateringly succulent.
It was a crooked deviation
       that I couldn't circumvent,
A kink incapable of being ironed straight.
How did my underage pelt illicit such carnage?
Such seething rage?

Confined by concrete gray, ice-cold eyes.
Evermore dwelling in a skeletal cell of weighted memory.
He roams free in the community,
       while I remain caged.

I'll never understand how a cherub could beseech
       such a brutalizing.
How an angel could be de-winged
Skewered,
Thrown on the grill,
And cheffed into a meal?

Is it really the steak's fault for being eaten?

(of course not)

A LIVING being slaughtered,
And for what?
A fleeting moment of pleasure?
Pleasure?
Nonconsensual pleasure.

Is it really the woman's fault for being raped?

(of course not)

Us women are reared in a society
    that favors facelessness.
Disembodied for the sake of the rapists.
Our mothers inseminated,
    birthing us into this world
        for our perceived purpose,
            a fleeting moment of pleasure.
Nonconsensual pleasure.

The hunters feel rightful,
    deserving and entitled.
Ordained by God himself
To conquest,
To pillage.
To start wars that have no end,
    a war against women.
We bear their children,
While they bear arms,
    their guns used against us.

These poachers never cease to hound us down.
Showering in the taboo of our endangered meat,
    even the meat they won't eat.
Discarded,
As a smoldering cigarette flicked from an open window.

Littering highway shoulders with our flesh,
Laid to rest in improvised graves.

The most dangerous game
    allows them to pay for play.
Buying erotic licensing to
Choke us,
    release,
        check our pulses,
Then pull the chord mercilessly
    until we are deceased.
This wicked hunger is no longer fueled
By the promise of a feast.
It has matured into a macabre itch to covet trophies.
Mantles decorated with dead deer heads,
Stuffed for display,
Posed in articulated contortions.
Memorialized as a reminder to our species,
That we are endangered
    on the verge of going extinct.
Haunting the vacant spaces once occupied
By optical organs,
Sits a staring set
    of somber glass eyes.
The hunters supplant the windows to our souls
As a final humiliation.
Removing the seeing
That saw the monster within the hunter.

Finding the weakest of the heard,
Targeting strays
    and runaways.
Hunters fulfill gaping fragility
    with the thrill of the kill.
These bestial men find it most appealing

To watch innocent beings
        stare up at the ceiling.
Incapacitated from being roofied.
Unable to move, we lay on our backs
        unfit to fight back.
They witness our spirits pour from our bodies.
Salty tears sprinting down
        devastated faces,
Condensed and titrated,
From the pressure of pitiful humping.
Forcibly funneled through our stillness.
To them,
        we taste sweeter than whiskey.
May you drown in consumption
From this fundamental perversion.

Meat eating is an ancient institution.
In a primordial time
        these men assembled sadistic syndicates.
Worshiping virility.
Birthing from their fruitless loins
A clandestine system built
        by the hunters,
                for the hunters.
A food chain hierarchy,
Deeply seeded in frangible masculinity.

Heterotrophic.
Surviving only
        by consuming others.
Allowing but a select few to ascend,
Becoming apex predators.
They could steal,
        they could mutilate,
                they could rape.

Unable to be hunted,
Impervious from being confronted.

These caped criminals began to find
There was no consequence for taking a life.
The slap on the wrist
      became a hushed whisper in the ear
            rather seductively.
Our omnipotent government,
Blinded by black robe blindfolds
Pulled over their faces,
Provides anonymity for the sake of plausible deniability.

The gavel never hits the bench.
Instead, they pass down subsidies
      to cattle ranchers that breed death,
            masked as food.
Pardons for rapists,
      masked as Supreme Court justices.

Where is the justice?

I refuse to believe our court's obsolete pro-life decree,
Because if they really gave a fuck
      about the babies in our society,
There would be no veal,
And
Rapists wouldn't walk free for cutting a deal.

The thing about all meat that you must remember,
Whether animal or human,
      it doesn't matter.
Before our clothes were removed,
      replaced by butcher paper wrapper.

Before we were carved,
    our pristine hymens cleaved.
Before we were laid on a dinner platter,
Remember that the meat you eat
    was once a living being
        who walked on two (four) feet.

Echoing from cribs, are the cries of society.
Eat, buy, don't question why.
Gangrenous from greed.
Stuffing pockets,
    stuffing faces,
        this is the American dream.
It's never enough.
Meanwhile the destiny of meat is predetermined,
Salted in suffering,
    seasoned to taste.
We are brined then basted,
And abruptly,
    senselessly,
        egregiously,
            unregretfully,
    our lives are ended,
    by the tip of lamentable dicks,
And the muzzles of smoking barrels.

Our knees are bloodied from pleading,
Bloodied from pleasing.

Some men condemn butchers
    and carnivores,
Begging their contemporaries to gag
    the need to feed
        this meat-eating cycle,
They stand in solidarity.

Refusing to normalize the behavior
Of those who illegally deflower,
    who unrightfully devour.
Our allies torch parasitic leeches
Before they suck the
    blood of childhood
        from young girls,
Eradicating the vampiric wrath of these cannibals.
We need more courageous men,
Kind men,
The ones that stand beside us women.

I daydream of these men,
But am haunted by nightmares of hunters.
Their future visits me as a premonition.
I envision a vengeful inescapable final destination,
Plotted by death itself.

Sleeping eyes flutter with satisfaction,
Gazing upon their descension
    into a raging inferno.
A vestibule of hell,
    too damned for Dante.
This is where wickedness will face judgment
    and damnation bestowed.
Karma will take what it is owed.

Their gluttonous mouths open wide
For a surreptitious kiss
    from the devil himself,
        a rapturous salutation
    sealed in thick spit.
Satan's tongue garners a sharp guarantee
Of an entrail episiotomy.
An obscene evacuation,

Scratched out with dirty nails of evil deeds.

Hemorrhaging.

Held together by a necktie noose,
Tightened by attempted evasion.
The tourniquet stops the bleeding
But constricts
        labored
                breathing.

Silence.

Stripped of all impetus,
Crimson-red saliva lines the lost contour
        of a destitute orifice,
With no lips, there are no words said.
At last,
These hunters are unable to call out our names,
        unable to victim blame.

I smell only the roasted remnants
Of a scolding malevolence
        frothing behind hollow rabid eyes.
No amount of cologne can disguise
The trojan plague that's rotting
        from the inside.
Pestilence is near, as the swarm of locusts form.
Mummified corpses are all that's left,
Shepherded to the afterlife by shit-eating flies,
Greed initiated this ceremonious demise.

They took,
        and took,
              and took,

Unrelentingly tempting fate.

But the scales have tipped,
No longer in the favor of the takers.
Oppression of the free is hereby absolved.
Those who have sought safety,
Cowering behind the monolith of patriarchy.
Watch it crumble
        as you are faced with a choice.
Crawl back into the ocean,
        or fucking evolve.

No need to hide.
No need to confess,
The world now knows your company lie.
"That the cow didn't matter,"
"That the girl was asking for it."

We demand our autonomy.
A non-meat-eating society.
Pronouncing our freedom from any kingdom
        who harbors a vendetta for bodily tyranny.

From this day forth
        all beings shall be treated equally.
Our safety upheld by the highest court,
The one who rules in favor of the hunted.
In favor of the ones
        who have already paid the highest price.
In favor of the ones
Who have paid with their lives.

The real reason I'm vegan
        is because I know what it's like
                to be eaten.

Restorative Injustice

They say I am a credible witness.
I query how they can substantiate my defensibility
     from something as arbitrary
         as my outwardly appearance.
What does my aesthetic denote?
That I am an appellant
     with an aptitude for honesty?
From mere vanity, they predetermined my ability
To withstand tenable trial demands.

They say I have a believable story
And testimonial fitness.
But, who decides which victims are worthy
     of taking the stand?
The authority to administer a litmus test,
Validating who among us deserves justice?

I venture to say that my hearsay
     will be admissible,
Pursuant to the following that I submit
     as indisputable evidence.
I'm white,
Educated
     and relatively attractive.
Well spoken,
     and reasonably non combative.

So they gave me a chance,
Because I look like their daughters.
This privilege was not born from happenstance.

Gathered round an oblong table with no end
Sits two probation officers,
    my mom, and husband.
Each scribbling notes,
Sandwiched between
    sighs and silences.

My every inhale
    and exhale being taped.
As I have to regale the tale,
    of the first time
        I was raped.

This briefing will undoubtedly be
    not so brief.
It's a muzzled memory,
Duct taped to the mouth of my history in silence.

They say healing is not linear,
    and while my gait runs straight
I will say,
There's truth in the skew of my trajectory.

Over hundreds of miles,
I haven't passed a single time trial.
Each mile marker reminding me
    of missing milestones.
Passed by each of my peers,
Who run unweighted,
    their feet take them
        in whatever direction they steer.
For they run without a snail's affliction.
Without the impulse to startle,
Shuddering back to shelled safety,
    they run without fear.

Each second spent wiping the sweat
        from my dripping brow,
The shame steeped in fatigue
        seeps deeper and deeper,
After carrying the faulted weight of this rape
        for what feels like decades.
Here,
My walk stops.

Unable to resist rigor mortise,
My body is overtaken by gravity,
        hopelessly limp.
Crashing down on cracked Colorado concrete,
In solidarity, my arteries crimp.
After thirteen years
I've run as far as I can from my assault.
The soles of my shoes,
Worn,
        bloodied with red.
The soul of my body,
        degraded
              and dead.
Ultra-marathoning breaks bodies,
Just as trauma
        when buried,
              ultimately buries you.
I guess what they say is true,
Because here I lie,
Watching myself die.

The sunrays wash over my body in waves,
Ritualistically embalming me.
The warmth feels like morphine,
        gifting me a brief rope of relief.
Decorated with blossomed poppies and posies,

Rock bottom has never smelled so sweet.
Only now do I grasp the grief
I swallowed when I was fifteen.

Ashes,
        ashes,
                I've taken my final fall.
This ring of secrecy
I've worn around my pinky,
This tarnished promise,
        finally dissolves.

Perhaps I should've stopped running
Before my heart turned blue.
I would've,
        but the night terrors wouldn't allow
                for my pace to slow,
                        for any forgiveness to grow.

The night sweats wouldn't relent in playing
Replays of my rapists' frightful faces.
Awoken.
Impeached from my sleep.
Rolling in pits of perspiration,
Drowning from fever fits.

That's why I'm here
        sitting at this table.
Puking up painful graphic details.
About who touched me first,
What they gave me to drink,
How they showered me off in between
        being inside of me.
Taking turns hacking at my hymen,
Splintering me in half

Sawing back and forth
        in synchronous sodomy.

The cops say,
"I'm sorry that happened to you."
But I can't hear their words
        or integrate their pity.
All I see are the tears welling in my mother's eyes.
As she is again for the second time,
Led in forced march
        down memory lane.
This time the trauma is not only mine to claim.

This is a means to an end,
An experimental new program
Called Restorative Justice.

Based out of Boulder,
Police officers hold space for victims
        to speak to their abusers.
Sit face to face,
And obtain some sort of closure.

With a goal to hold them liable,
Show them that the perpetrated abuse is undeniable.
Stitch their eyes open,
        and stuff their ears
                with years
                        of guilt-ridden tears.

An invitation was mailed to his house.
I wanted the robber of my virginity to know,
Hurt cannot be insured.
There was no policy that protected
The vulnerable parts inside of me.

My claim is valid,
But the only payout I received via mail
Was a return to sender, his gagged refusal.

He can reject my plea
To listen.
But what I cannot allow
Is for his continued spewing
      of a story so fictitious,
Untethered to a single shred of reality.

Let's let the court summon his appearance.
Warrant his arraignment.
A jury of peers can deliberate his destiny.
The district attorney agrees with me.
She says, that with her expertise
      she guarantees a litigious finale.
I beg her to max him out
      like a credit card,
After racking up thirteen years of interest,
It's time he faces the charge.

The police officer assigned to my investigation,
      told me "we all make mistakes."
As if insinuating
      the rape was MY mistake.
As if, it were against guy code
To question another man's predation.

That it was I
      who put myself
           in a bad situation.
Therefore the outreached clutch
That gripped me from the tree of purity,
Was rightful in eating such a low-hanging fruit.

Mr. Officer then private messaged me about astrology,
Asking me about my sign,
Messaging, for any reason he could find.
It doesn't take a psychic to predict his tactic
In working with survivors
      is to intimidate,
            and invalidate their rape.
Slather them in romantic advances,
Persuasively extorting dates.

I reported this adulteration of trust,
Only to attend a funeral for justice.
Where black widows peer through tinted hearse windows,
Crossing fingers for a resurrection.
Her casket stained crimson,
The six-foot hole swallows her whole.
My tears stand to say a few words,
A eulogy,
A plea,
For a postmortem apology.

Justice is dead.

May she rest in pieces.

Their search and seizure tactics
Devolved into
Search and seize-her antics.

Prosecute?
Mr. Officer prefers to persecute by
Victim blaming and shaming.
Unflinching in his tact,
This wasn't his first time

Betraying the badge,
        and likely not his last.

The loyalty they claim,
To protect their community.
They must be bluffing
        because you know what happened to Mr. Officer,
Fucking nothing.

When does a defender
Actually defend her?
Without trying to sleep with her.
Pillars of protection, erected to keep us safe
Buckle under weighted blue vests
        of alleged integrity.
When the police force is allowed
To exert their force,
They fail to uphold liberty.

They said I would be a reliable witness,
        but the hands struck ten
                the clock has run out.

My goal to hold you culpable
Continues to be curtailed.
Having a ten year statute of limitations
        on sexual assault is an absolute fail.

Now they say there's not enough evidence.
The veneer of belief has been eaten away.
An acidic reaction,
Yielded neutralization.
In the absence of proof
The district attorney bubbles up
        with a fearful trepidation to intervene.

My story became a convoluted knot of misplaced faith,
Caught in the cogs of our legal mechanism.
The gears,
Lubricated by the blood of our ancestors.
From the survivors of racism,
                        sexism,
                  classism,
          and ableism.
From all of us who have come forward.

My file now lives amongst a stack of anonymous victims.
All silenced
      by systematic violence.
Fucked over by institutional compliance.
This machine was not built
      for the good of our country.
This is not the land of the free,
      unless your identity is an
           old,
                  white,
                        he.
Am I not privileged enough to be believed?
Privileged enough to feel
      the fair face of justness?

Sick from emotion,
I cry every time I think about the countless victims
      who are forced to disappear.
Coerced to drop their motions.
Forced to yield cases,
Forsake reports of violence
For we all know
           prosecutors will vacate it.
Hospitals perform rape kits, but never submit

Because there's no question
         of where they're destined to go,
                  stashed on a shelf
                           and left to sit.

Sole survivors,
Our identities are stripped away
By character assassinations made off-hand.
Whispers of "whore" echo,
         through courthouse halls.
Represented on dockets by nameless numbers,
Abandoned before we even hit the witness stand.

How can a system that retraumatizes
         and revictimizes
Pledge even the illusion of justice?

It's madness.

They told me,
"Your rapist is living a miserable life."
Like that's supposed to solidify
         even an ounce of solace.
How does that provide recompense
For all the years he lived free, at my expense.

I told them "No."
Let the clarity of my voice be unquestioned
         in its absolution.
The only judicious restitution
That could be wielded by a fair court,
         would be handing down an order
                  of execution.

Not an ending of his life,
 but an ending of abuse.

It's not asking for too much,
To execute his freedom.
Once locked in prison,
He can no longer procure virgins.
And he can take his turn
 as the recipient
  of unwanted touch.

That didn't happen.
He didn't go to jail,
 at least not because of me.
Years later he was found guilty.
The charge,
 he sexually defiled a child.
In my case, the leniency he received,
 is the reality survivors expect.
The courts preserved his freedom,
Simultaneously thieving me of mine.
After years of suppression
My mind was overtaken by curiosity.
So I searched his name
 in the sex offender registry.
Staring at me, from across the screen
An address,
An atrocity,
He lives 6.9 miles away from me.

The end.

It's not the ending I deserve, but it does serve as a conclusion.
My story may not be entirely deposed,

But this chapter feels completely written
      and is ready to be closed.

Can justice really ever be restored?
As women,
      we are reminded at the graveyard.
The inscription scribbled upon the tombstone of Lady Justice,
Still asks,
"Was she a reliable witness?"

Narcissist-itis

A stringent inflammation from ego inflation.
In a medical sense,
It's an irreversible deformity of one's
       self-awareness.

No need to dispense a test
       to identify the infected.
Those who are positive
Are carriers of a mirror in each pocket.
Their brain craves to cure the pain
With ample self-appreciation.
You'd think the repetition of incessantly
Seeing their own faces refracted
Would precipitate some quantifiable
       self-reflection.

No, that would require scrutiny
       of their outwardly presenting perfection.
Those diseased simply cannot be expected
To magnify anything inside
That could call to question
       their self-glorification.

Coming from an expert on the matter,
I can tell you without hesitation
What hurts more than their shit filled
       superficial constipation,
Is the grief endured by their family
From imposed pathological friction.

Rubbing us raw,
Indignantly gifting a rash
      of poisonous annoyance.
What starts as a raised textured itch
Builds into an anaphylactic infuriation
From never earning a spot in their trophy case.
For the reality is,
That we will always come in second place.

Some days my heart still aches,
As it tries to decide
      why I am so hard
           for you to love.
In the interim of formulating an answer
I sloppily paste a smile on my face.
Supposing your irreverence
      will never know it's fake,
Because you fail to see,
The collateral hostages that exist
      in your periphery.

You fear acknowledging my sadness
Will take attention away
      from your morose misery.
So you don't.
Don't see me.
      don't hear me.
           don't know me.

You might've fertilized my existence,
But the moment I was suctioned
      from my mother's uterus,
You cut the cord of obligation.

No longer tied to the humorous notion
        that another person's needs
                could come before yours,
                        not even your own creations'.
That day, your empathy's disguise became paper-thin,
For in your heart,
        only you can win.

So as we gather round the dinner table,
We are surrounded by the cacophony
        of your depressive autobiography.
Pounding against the drum of our ears
You recite a meticulous list of discontentment,
Starting with the job you hated,
        but chose to keep for twenty years.
Then comes the criticism of women,
How they should all be skinny,
And not easily offended,
        so that when you joke about rape
                they laugh at what you said.
You can't stand snowflakes,
        especially the ones that threaten
                your automatic weapons.
Resenting the baby girl you got, when you clearly asked for a son.
Victimized by circumstance,
Gratitude seemingly skipped a generation.
You say life is unfair,
        but you're just unfulfilled.
To offset insecurity,
        you make us all feel inadequate.
You want more, but don't appreciate what you have.
Contentment doesn't evade you, you killed it.

I wish for an antidote,
Something to counteract this venomous outlook.
I wish you could see the beauty in life,
     and the beauty in me.

But perhaps hope for a cure
Is a bit premature,
For all I can hear
     is the ring of echoed tinnitus
From your profound case of narcissist-itis.

Flower Power

Here's to seeing beauty
        in the stage before the bloom.
We all like to be seen,
But first,
        pause and feel.
Acknowledge, and give thanks to the ingredients
That allowed for you to heal.

The road to spring cannot be rushed,
        for winter is essential preparation
                for impending propagation.

This season before the bloom is often gray,
        and overwhelmed by rain.
They are hard earned days.
We wish to fast-forward
        to the summer sun.
Our perennial stalks empty and withered,
        pray for future rays.

Breathe in, and realize
That you were made to withstand all seasons of life.
That flowering is fleeting,
        and you can acclimatize
                to any condition
                        you may find yourself in.

Here's to the souls,
That've been uprooted,
Who survived a ground shaking upheaval.
To those who thwarted frigid bouts.
Knowing their value is not measured

By the amount of petals they sprout,
But by their resilience,
      and that against winter's winds,
          they grew.
The stage before the bloom,
    is just for you.

You Had Me At Cello

There's nothing like
The feeling of creating music.
What unfolds between paper-thin sheets
    ignites an inner awakening.
Each instrument,
    a gratifying undertaking.
There's only one
I've never had the pleasure of playing.

She dances on stage with the orchestral ensemble,
While I stand at attention at the back of the auditorium,
    grappling with my attraction.
What starts as a slight tremble
Initiates an exothermic reaction,
My heart palpitating,
    skin yearning,
        my mouth salivating.

Surveying her hourglass silhouette
Saturates me with gay fascination.
Instinctively I know,
We are destined to perform a duet,
    a euphoric concerto.

She has been handcrafted by the ultimate artisan.
The obligation I now vow
Is to play her the way she rightfully deserves,
    with acclaim,
        and unhinged adoration.

Unblemished,
Not a hint of warping in sight.

She's tuned to perfect fifths,
Each peg wound
      erotically tight.

Atop her head sits a logarithmic scroll,
Spiraled into a single Botticelli curl.
A sculpted crown,
      fitting for the queen of queens,
            superbly embellishing the woman of my dreams.

A true masterpiece,
Forged of maple and spruce.
One of a kind,
Unable to be imitated
      or reproduced.

Oh, Calypso, you captivate me so.
I admit, I'm obsessed.
You are indeed the goddess
      of strange power.
Musically seducing all those who hear you,
A siren of sexual mercy.

So I grasp her bow.
Settling into the nature of its ergonomic curvature.
Softening it with each turn
      of my waterlogged fingers,
            I undo the verve that's been pent
                  into her tension screw.
She falls free,
Each strand of bound brown hair
Cascades pendulously,
      sticky from lusty rosin debris.

She thirsts
    for acoustic undulation.
So my fingers articulate to full extension.
Surfing her fingerboard.
Back and forth,
She trills with appreciation
    as I pluck.

A more pleasurable sound has never been produced by Pizzicato.
She aches to be played,
    I ache to obey.
Her body sublimely nestled between my legs,
Buzzing from vibrato.
Each of my thigh muscles contract
    to grip her in place
        and make her stay.

Ignoring the metronome prompt,
    as it ticks away.
With each measure
    our cadence falls
        further astray.
Getting ahead of ourselves, faster and faster.
Our timing is climbing,
    as her strings are throbbing
        preparing for a high octave shriek.

After hours of play,
Sweat begins to sprint.
She's slipping,
But I refuse to allow the music to cease.

Swiftly, I grasp her prolonged swan neck.
She arches back in a sway,
A windless gasp strikes her crescendo,

Her diaphragm reverberating
        as she bellows on forte.
A creature swells and comes cracking
Through her wooden chest.
What escapes is a beguiling songbird,
Singing a sultry song
        that I've never before heard.
Yet somehow I sing along,
Because I too
        know all the words.

Her leg quivers
        and gives out.
I bend to retrieve her.
Numerable pages of the score
        come crashing to the floor.

This feeling of creating music.
The release,
        there's nothing like it.
Between paper thin sheets, I find myself.
Not in love with her taste,
        but lustful for the flavor of play.

I don't mean to offend her,
But what gets me off most is the fact
        that music knows no gender.
It's the free drug
That makes you feel
        doped up and high.
Music doesn't give a fuck if you're bi.

Identity Cry-Sis

Have you ever made a life-altering decision
That was perfectly timed?
Maybe there's no such thing,
      but since they say timing is everything,
Admittedly, I tried.
On the calendar I marked the day
      in which I would emancipate my Pride.

Once broken, news cannot be undone or unspoken.
Like origami,
      how it unfolds is always a mystery.
The release date was properly aligned.
Like I said,
Perfectly timed.
June 28th, 2022,
      I double-checked,
It was ordained by the new moon.
Who am I to ignore the endorsement
      of an astrological sign?
The moon said,
"Girl, unlike me, this isn't a phase for you.
      this new cycle represents a new true you."
With my readiness and stars in harmony,
I accepted my summons,
      finally ready to let the world see
            all
                  of
                       me.
The universe said,
It's GO time!

I sprawled out my vulnerability

For everyone to see,
"Hi, I'm Bi."
That was it, short and sweet.
Of course,
       in a rhyme.
It wasn't terribly elaborate,
Certainly no points for creativity,
       but the messaging
             felt complete.

Upon hitting post, I felt a rush of normalcy.
That posting about my sexuality was no different
Than sharing a picture of a plant,
       or my latest vegan recipe.

Given my privilege,
I assumed the majority of my circle would be kind,
They're mostly liberal,
       and of a similar mind.
I prepared my nerves for a few rolling eyes,
Expecting the rumor mill
       to strike family tabloids.
The grapevine loves to spill tea,
It was only a matter of time before
Sour juice was extracted from my story,
       and used to ferment a scandalous wine.
But the bottle was dry.
Responses were sparse,
       only a drop of likes.
Then a cup of remarks,
       broken over my head,
            with sharpened shards,
                 aimed straight at my heart.

"Is this a joke?" She says.

No,
        it's just me,
My unmasked identity.

Scarlet droplets stain my suspense-bitten lip.
Her portending moment of pause,
Swiftly plunges into a septic skepticism.
Swirling suspicion,
Strong enough to make
        even a cynic's stomach sick.
As someone who flies the flag of feminism,
I assumed you'd be the first to pick me up,
        not the scrapper to boot me down.
Hooking my name to your hitch
        and dragging it around.

Everyone else was quiet.

I guess people don't know what to say,
        when you tell them you're gay, or queer, or bi.
But for future reference,
Silence hurts more than any other reply.
It would have been easier to hear angry screams,
        told to kick rocks and die.
Because lack of feedback
Makes me question if I even came out at all.
Or if my existence counts,
        I've never felt so small.
This quiet denial
        has plunged me into a pit of isolation
                and made me a bit suicidal,
I just want to cry-sis.

Society's general vibe suggests Queerness is an illness,
Indicative of a public health crisis.

They fear that bi-ness
        could rabidly jump up and bite,
Infecting straights
      with a gayness
           inducing virus.
Making a hug, or overt compassion
A risky behavior.
The media declares that contracting this contagion
Happens when in close proximity,
       people are told to avoid those
            with a differing sexuality.

If you're a woman,
Same sex attraction is radical in college,
All the boys flock to watch.
Being bi is fine for a short time,
But once you've aged out of the male gaze,
It's no longer fine?

Sharpie scribbled as gospel in bathroom stalls
Preaches a reckoning for those who refuse to choose.
These toilet throned crusaders categorize bisexuals as confused.
Greedy,
      a threat to monogamy
           and unable to make up our minds.
So we exist on the periphery.
Never straight enough,
Nor gay enough,
For our queerness
      to be taken seriously.

"Don't ask, don't tell,"
Is not a reasonable request.
For exposing trueness
Cannot idly be postponed as the adage suggests.

Not for a lifetime,
       a month,
              or even another minute.
Crawling back into the closet
Doesn't keep us hidden,
It slams the door on possible happiness,
Confined to our minds.
Cloistered by lies
       impossibly depressed.

How many intrepid souls
Have felt this chokehold of misery?
Murdered by the holy penalty,
       found guilty,
             but only of being true
       to their identity.
Lines of lovers waiting at will call,
Forced to admire
       from an eclipsed distance.
Lost,
       never requited.

Open your mind,
Before you open your mouth.
When viewed through a lens of acceptance,
It's our chiral sameness
       that you'll witness.

I forgive myself,
       for thinking that I exist for enjoyment.
I forgive you,
       for thinking that I exist for judgment.

Homegrown homophobia.
Plotted by the colonizers who claimed land,

         people,
                  culture,
                           and color.
Forced pilgrimages.
Bloody hands shake on a deal of heteronormativity.
Gutted,
The grounds we water with tears,
         were tilled with instruments of fear.
Seedlings sprayed with pesticidal propaganda.
Those who threaten ideology,
         are the first to be tagged,
                  and body bagged,
Laid in a marginalized line at the cemetery gates.
There they wait.

Every June,
         they erupt in revulsion.
Femurs and ribs poke up at despicable feet,
Reminding gravediggers,
         that they cannot bury people alive
And hatred cannot consign an entire community
         to the ash heap of history.

To be gay is to be demonized,
         to be bi is to be fetishized,
                  to be human is to love.
Love
         is
                  love.

We deserve Pride,
         not homicide.

This is a crisis—
         and it makes me want to cry-sis.

Granular Discomfort

Become devoted
        to the granular,
That which doesn't glide,
Nor ripen,
That which intends its gruff
        and whiskered danger.

Cherish the untidy,
The ulcerated underbelly,
Where pain grapples with pleasure
And desire is met with ruthless anxiety.

Release into the intimate wetness
        of an unnamed stranger.
Unclasp your palms,
        allow them to pant.
May they drown in sweat
        from the heat of not knowing
              what's coming next.
Smell the transient dalliance
Sworn by the heat of their breath
        on the nape of your neck.

Witness their soft scented wax
        drip upon your wide open chest.
Permit it to puddle.
Encourage it to run from conscious concern
        with unflinching distress.
Feel your skin burn.

Revel in each pebble
That seizes the sole

of your naked foot.
Assured that your heel will heal,
Thicker than before.
Uneven and course
        from being cut open,
                left to fester,
      in putrid beauty.
Savor the seduction of being sore.

Bathe in the riddled conundrum
        of an untilled minefield,

Studded with incendiary   uncertainty.

Each step you steal,
Each questionable box you select,
Allow your mind
To become mindswept.

This mortal game we all play,
        we'll eventually lose.
Making each second spent living
A wagered risk.

Forbid fear from reaping enjoyment
        from what has yet to happen.
Embargo its ability to restrict,
For fear will always attempt to tame the volatility
That's born from unknown possibilities.

Without trepidation,
Frolic in the fatal mystery
        that is
                the human condition.

Scale the barbed fence,
Lined with warning signs.
Be drafted by whatever bellows your name.
Dance in the crosshairs
    of another's aim.
Take the chance.
For each survived invasion,
    you fortify your tolerance.

Drink down the unsightly grit
That's tucked under your lovers' nail beds.
Lick the boundary
    of their compulsory affliction.
The junction,
    where skin meets anxiety's teeth.
All ten, bitten to the quick.

Trust there is a clumsy perfection to an untied shoe.
A sensual abhorrence to a blistered soul,
    that's been shaken
        to the point of submission.

Tell me how you crave the complication,
That which needs, and wants,
That which knows only
    how to misbehave.
I live bridled to this pain,
    it yokes me.
Shackled to the vow of destruction,
    it chokes me.
The real reason I ride hardest when I hurt,
Is to trick sensations.
By using pain as foreplay
    I can cum
        from discomfort.

No

I tried it on,
        but it didn't fit me.
A defective retort
That was heard as a request for more.
A sword that's lost its sharp.
A word that's uttered by ungrateful whores.

No,
Sounds so rude.
In its absence,
My muted distress and broken zipper
Are misread as a yes.
Feigned consent slithers in one ear
And through to the next.

I know that No still lives somewhere inside me,
In a place that's not been touched
By the flesh of men.

No.
He rolls me over,
Shoving himself in the wrong hole.
My No is afraid to correct him,
        my silence is praised
                and he sends me on my way.

Buried Treasure

A great teacher is an excavator.
With fastidious precision
She brushes away furrowed sediment
    grain by grain.
With her ear to the Earth,
    she witnesses our plight,
        and listens.

Saturating surrounding rivers
With mistful maternal tears.
Her fluvial tides douse barren deserts,
Until the land slushes beneath calloused feet,
Gushing from sacred surges.
An emotional flash flood,
    she rains
        with the wetness of her love.
Birthing through her canal
    an unstoppable upheaval.
Overwhelming the burden of leaden clay,
Washing it away.

Liberating our buried treasure from the dust.
Salvaging brittle bodies,
    baked into soil.
Releasing our encrusted mummified
    hopes from catacomb crypts,
Where eternity was bound to swallow us
    entirely.

The grit of her resolve
Unearths shattered pieces of us.

Pieces, buried and ignored,
    eclipsed by the brutality of time.
A treasure hunter of sorts,
She heard the call from historical relics,
    threatening to dissolve.
Returning day after day
To the fields of sand and palm,
    where shimmering dunes reflect
        a web of waterways.
An oasis,
Where murky rivers tether century-old trees to umbilical lifelines,
    nurturing them as Nile guardians.
As overseers of wind-blown ridges,
They stand as Bastet,
The goddesses of protection and pleasure,
Daughters of the sun.

Guided by unwavering celestial circling,
Her trajectory is an unfaltering orbit.
No matter the weather,
    sunshine or torrential gloom,
Steady as the rising tide,
    our teacher stands watch at our side.
Her loyalty is to the bulbs yet to bloom.
Her sworn oath,
Steeped in resolution
    to never cease progress,
        until our greatness
            is no longer entombed.

Until then,
Knee deep in this mess,
    among the lotus
        is where she will reside.
Hovering above our preserved potential,

She eats away at caked
        sedimentary soil.
This is the Valley of the Queens,
Where we lay slain.
Where our gilded crowns have been stowed
        waiting to be freed.
Freed,
        not pillaged or unrightfully claimed.
Stolen,
Sold as souvenirs.
Appropriated ownership
        of our quarried antiquities,
              sold to fund colonial loans.

She protects us from this thievery,
From being raided without consent.

Singularly sovereign.

Unchaining our womanly autonomy.
Uncovering riches of expertise,
Self-efficacy,
Femininity.
Introduced as strangers
        to the movement of our pelvis,
              stumbling from the sheer capability
                  of our anatomy.
She educates us on instinctual readiness,
The reflex we each possess,
        to be rebellious.

A great teacher is a shapeshifter.
Our restoration,
Shepherded by wisdom and context.
She collects our splintered shards.

Reassembling the fragments,
    with glue,
        screws,
            and a kiss of brilliance.
Knitting a tapestry of metamorphosis.
Drawing into our skin,
    hymns of perseverance.
Cocooning us with vibrant hues.
Patterning us in storytelling.
Branding us with sacred tattoos.
Reinforcing our bones with resilience,
    rebar and plaster.
Our posture, erect.
    harder than before.
Unyielding yet flexible,
With winged projections
    outstretched in confidence.
Because of her
    we are stronger.

A great teacher is a great student.

Listening for foreign tongue, to speak back words that affirm.
Studying the origin of suffering, to better befriend glee.
Dancing circles around a crucible of cultural celebration.
She speeds in a blazing pursuit of education,
    baptized as a global citizen.
Bitten with a proclivity to assimilate her mastery,
    integrating past and present.
She seeks
    only to liberate.

Buried wealth
Is returned to its rightful owners,
Us.

The pale veil of patriarchy has been removed.
Our faith, reinstated,
As if opening our eyes for the first time,
Squinting to regain vision,
We see
        our valor to rise.

A great teacher is a linguistic luminary,
Fluent in the colloquial tongue of rebellion.
She translates the lasting lineage of our ancestors,
Reviving the drum of deep seeded rhythms.
Speaking first with song,
        then echoed by dance,
As women, we lead the revolutionary chant.

We no longer answer,
        to those who say we can't.
To those who scorch the Earth beneath us,
        as if scorned by our existence.
We condemn those who seek to keep us caged.
Castigate the men who abuse their power,
Who are threatened by our hair
        that goes uncovered.
We no longer cower,
Under the obelisk shadow
        that's cast by their outrage.

We are grateful to our teacher.
For exposing our capacity
        to overthrow unjustly control.
Because of her,
We are free.
Free to engineer our futures,
        and actualize our dreams.
Manifest a new destiny.

Armed with our crowns,
We reign with the wetness of love,
Birthing through our canals
      an unstoppable upheaval.
Overwhelming the burden of those who once stood over us,
We now dance on their graves,
Washing their fanatical bigotry away.

Our greatest teacher is a resistor.

Scrolling

Mindless finger wagging,
May result in
      meme hoarding,
           internet trolling
                and thirst traps.
Addicted to the tick of notifications,
Bated into distraction,
One like causes a dopamine spike,
Instant relapse.

It mainlines us with our favorite vices,
      shopping,
           porn,
                mating,
                    and more.
We ignore what's actually in front of us.
Emancipating the need to interact,
We make love to our phones,
It scans our eyes,
      while we look deep
           into its screen.
This is more dangerous than it seems.

Send Noods

The drool rolling down your chin
Scrounges to find a plate of sustenance to burrow in.
So you order up a bowl of innocence,
Slurping mangled morsels,
      devouring each individual pixel.

This must be your secret to a youthful appearance,
The hot steam arising from a curated bowl of underage noods
Provides you with a facial improperly taboo,
      leaving you damned
           but renewed.

I left you unread
But I didn't forget,
      you just texted again,
           begging to know
                my specials of the night.
So we mentally wrestle until we're saturated in sweat.
You roll my revulsion
      back and forth in your mouth.
Scrapping and brawling.
Relishing the spice of my fight,
      it's my resistance that gets your underwear wet.
Flavoring your words with flattery,
You speak me into submission
By dousing me with compliments
      buttering me copiously,
           until I offer
      a hesitant consent.

The bell is rung,
I lost this fight to your silver tongue,

Eventually hitting send.
I'm immediately hit with a gut punch of regret,
When it comes to your redundant hunger
    there's simply no end.

You demand to be fed,
Eating first with your eyes.
No matter how many bowls I serve up,
    you refuse to be denied.

So I remove the plastic wrapping
    that adorns my nude,
Lay on my bed and click the shutter repeatedly,
Frame by frame,
    I shudder repeatedly.
With each picture,
I fall further from the focus of modesty,
Contorting my naughty body.
Serving up my curves as a plate of hor d'oeuvres,
Securing the raw exposures,
    that you scarcely deserve.

The dawn of my desire to please,
Was taught by a cookbook quite deviant indeed,
It latched on to my purity,
    claiming me as a virginal devotee.
Priming me with a famishing need to feed.
This book of recipes was gratuitously gifted to me,
By a chef with unquestionable expertise.

He force-fed me my first nood,
    like a good girl,
        I choked it down,
His name was Chris,

A massage therapist
        from a small mountain town.
He was between thirty-five and forty,
And I might've looked older,
        but I was only thirteen.

He got my number,
        and willingly confessed
That while massaging me,
His fingers were palpating each morsel of my pre-teen body.
He swore that his mind fantasized
        about doing much more.
He professed in bristled detail,
What he would've done
        had my mom not been
                in the room next door.

This prick slathered it on thick,
Corrupting me with a single file of steaming hot noods.
Pleasuring himself to the thought of my taste.
Dredging his dick on full display,
Force-feeding my eyes a pornographic buffet.
Basting himself in his own fatty juices,
And I couldn't look away.
My thoughts began to spiral,
        as I mistook his hunger for infatuation,
But behind that spa uniform
        and surreptitious smile
                stood a rancid pedophile.

Over many moons and many meals,
I became accustomed to being groomed,
        conditioned to being consumed.

Confidence, a key absent ingredient.
So I used the words of strangers
       to soothe old wounds
              from daddy's damage.
I would do what I was instructed to do.
Butterfly my carcass,
Lying askew upon a digital platter.
Poised for attention,
Offering up my dignity to whoever would eat me.
Who the eater was, didn't matter.
This continued
Until I stopped
       giving food away
             for free.

Orders from strangers
Are distastefully rude.
And noods are not food,
They are ammunition
       that can be weaponized
              by people you date,
Used by pedophiles for self-pleasure,
Used by those with a vengeful ache.
When our bodies are pixelated
Our future is diced into hundreds of pieces.
The outcome is unclear,
       the risk is severe.

We surmise safety when hiding
       behind a screen,
Assuming a layer of technological protection,
But humans are much more dangerous than they seem.
Embedding like a virus in our cells,
Manipulating the most vulnerable parts of ourselves.

So let's start a new trend,
Leave thirsty texts unread.
Ignore their desperate attempts to be fed,
And think twice before hitting send.

The real reason they use hunger as an excuse,
Is to justify their abuse.
Juicing you up,
        to drink your youth.

A Won Woman Army

We tread down the streets in a hurry,
Zigzagging and weaving,
Crossing at the end of each block.
As women,
        we don't have the privilege
                of taking a leisurely walk,
We scurry.
Feeling their piercing eyes
Keenly keeping up with us,
        as they stalk.

Passing by a sister in arms,
We wave,
Glancing at each other's wrists.
Seeing a shared savage accessory,
Metal spiked talons protruding from our fists.
Homemade brass knuckles
        discreetly woven
                from a barbed set of car keys.
I thought it was only me,
Born with a mistrust of the Male Militia.
But I guess this fear is ubiquitous with having a uterus.

My face appears pale from this clenching,
        though I assure you,
                my glare is unflinching.
A one-woman platoon.
Shielding my figure with baggy gear,
Swaddling my flesh in a clothing cocoon.
From childhood it was implanted in me
        that showing skin is menacing.

Taught that my looks come with consequence,
      I bear the responsibility
           to always beware.
So I conceal my breasts
With my dad's bulletproof vest.
Layering on long pants and a turtleneck,
      so that no one could suggest,
That the sight of my skin
      declared warfare.

Where do I reside?
The streets of the Middle East?
News outlets pour salt in the female wound
Exclaiming that autonomy doesn't exist
      because of extremist terrorists.
The Western world gasps in horror
With a pernicious uproar that the war
      on women's rights persists.
But I beg you to do a double take,
Peer to the patch on my uniformed arm,
There you will see,
Stitched on as swag is an American flag,
This is America.

Where women race to their cars,
Locking doors with maddening pace.
Where fragile masculinity
      is loaded into shelled artillery.
Safeguarded by the second amendment,
We are gunned down in mass quantity,
This is the land of the free.

America,
Where women bear the brunt of violence.
Misogyny shoulders us with suicide vests of cortisol.

Reaped by a silent killer,
The sword of the assassin is heart disease.
Strained from being born into battle,
Constantly oppressed,
        and the shell shock of endless unrest.

As women, we are not guaranteed
Life, liberty, and safety
        in this land of opportunity.
In this land, are we free?

Three women a day, fall slain.

Choked by the loving hands of lovers and husbands.
Makeup cannot conceal the bruise of death,
Our bodies lay limp
        at the bottom of the stairs,
Leaving our mark, as an everlasting carpet stain.

Survival is bleak.
Jaws of steel are born from clenching.
Gritting our teeth to the gum,
As our bodies fall victim to torturous war crimes
Again and again.
Sexual violence is a guarantee.
We can run,
        but its reach is all-encompassing,
Our mothers,
        our sisters,
                our daughters and friends.
Raped.
The women who brush up against you in the street,
        the majority of the women you'll meet.
Raped.

Can we ever escape?

They wage war with half the population
To elicit the prized commodity
 stowed between our legs.
The gush of our crude oil is their salvation.
They want to bathe in it,
 without having to beg for it.
So they construct pipelines to profit from us fiscally.

Wanted dead or alive,
 women are the world's biggest industry.

Men pine for power,
So they mine our resources
 sending in entire infantries.
This is an age-old tactic used to justify their heinous acts,
These are homegrown terrorists.
Fracking us,
 raping us,
 impregnating us.
Then regulating our uteruses,
Forcing births,
 securing our enslavement in poverty.
Only to shoot us dead
 for peacefully protesting
 on their government property.

In my mind I formulate a future horizon,
Asking the question
 what if us women won for once?
I see a mirage of freedom,
 a moment of elation,
 when I no longer

       have to carry my tampons
Next to my handgun.

On this day,
I am not a one-woman army.
It's no longer necessary
       to compulsively look behind me,
             back and forth to each side,
Or in the car before I slide inside.
Our neighborhoods have finally qualified
       to be demilitarized.
So I walk slowly,
       along the road near my home.
Take my son to the park and swing.
We close our eyes
       for the first time.
Without the fear of opening them
To an unwanted surprise.
Knowing the war is over.
The real reason,
       a smile dances across my face,
I can finally see a world where
Women are allowed to survive.

Erosion

The science of surrendering,
        the worship of kneeling.
Gazing up with appreciation.
Opening to the sky with no expectations.
Welcoming each kiss of rain,
        on your face
              with dogmatic adoration.
This is how a rock undergoes erosion.

With grace,
        humble acceptance.
Yet, the human experience is expressed otherwise.
Typically characterized
        by a fickle resistance.

We fall into the trap set by our frontal lobes,
By our thinking that we can preserve
        these mortal bodies indefinitely.

We desire certainty,
Aspiring to predict the future.
To prevent heartache.
To resist the scathing weather.

From the moment we are born,
With outstretched fingers
        of nature's abrasion
              we are welcomed.

Surrounded by the storm.

Baptismally dunked into the water of our ancestors.

Entirely submerged.

The instant we learn to fear death,
We draw our swords.
But to fight the wind
        is not a war that we can win.
Fall to defeat,
Abandon the need to fight mortality.
Only then can you access a sacred alchemy
That renders evolved beings.

Earth,
        Water,
              Wind,
                      and Fire.

This is the nursery where nature's fury
Explores each enclave
        of the human form.
Here, death does not exist.
We are indeed
Merely,
        changed by the storm.

Exposed.
        Stripped.
              Sculpted.

Torrential weather
Withers on the fringes
        of our frayed edges.
Carving canyons
        and deep basins.
These hollowed pits allow us
To carry more.

More heartbreak,
        more joy,
                more mistakes.

As we succumb to the crumble
Letting go,
        allowing for change,
We extend forth an invitation
For the universe to merge our creation
        with our destruction,
                this is how stars are born.

These merciless winds of change require sacrifice.
A chemical peel of our exteriors,
A melting
        of our primordial glacial accumulation.

Just as the mountains
        become rocks,
               become sand,
Our surface area increases
        as we expand.
We erode,
So that we can grow.

We Are Enough

We are women.
The womb that bestows life,
    the heart that all call home.
Cradling the world in our cosmic gravity,
Knowing when to hold on,
    and when to let go.

We breathe the ancestral air of women
    who have come before us.
The poets,
The scientists,
The mothers,
The warriors,
The innovators,
The protectors.
We inherit their collective trauma,
    and inhale their collective joy.
Respiring a purified exhalation for the next generation.

We come from a lineage of injury,
Wanting to stay soft, while needing to be tough.
We honor our history,
    by pushing boundaries.
We are women,
    we are enough.

5:55

The precise moment you arrived Earthside.
Laying on my naked chest,
You took your first sips of life from my breast.
5:55 was your birth time,
    and it was also mine.

As a child myself,
Conceiving at eighteen,
    young and afraid,
        we grew up together.
Crying in each other's arms,
Swaddled in a shared heartbeat.
Assured of one thing,
That being your mother,
    would always be
        my most worthwhile endeavor.

555 means change,
Transition,
    adventure,
        a cosmic sign to keep an open mind.

Your soul brought with it, an omen of discovery.
Powering our momentum to vanquish adversity,
We latched onto love and never let go.

You are the real reason I'm alive,
    I survived to be by your side.

Home Is Where the Hospital Is

A snake of plastic tubing constricts in my fists,
    wrapping concentric circles,
        strangling my pinky.
This is how a masochist distracts from the harsh paddle of reality.
A needle fangs itself into tired veins,
At this point,
    I don't even bleed
        I just leak.
My nose chokes on the sterile plastic smell
That's threading itself from my nostrils
    down my throat,
Curling up in the bowels of my stomach,
It feels right at home,
    and my gag knows this scent well,
        this is the smell of the hospital.

A medicinal peppering
Sets my cheeks ablaze with a feverish heat,
As saline minerality
Floods an ocean from my blood to my mouth.

The opioids
    pin my eyes,
        leaving me paralyzed.
Is this the taste of wellness
    or sickness?
I'm too high to notice.

Leeches in lab coats suck me dry,
Sacrificing my wetness to the syringe,
I no longer recoil,

or flinch
        or cringe.
I am a patient who has lost all of my patience,
    at my wits' end.

I have been failed by Western medicine.
Abandoned in this hospital,
Sane but unstable,
To white coats and white walls,
    we're all the same.
A number,
    no name,
        a hypochondriac,
            a burden to blame.

Our world was not built for differently abled bodies.
This was made clear to me
    when using my wheelchair.
I felt the glare of judgmental stares,
    as they slammed doors in front of me.
I counted how many stairs there are in this damn city.
Do they expect us to climb?
From a seated position, I was able to see
    how little society cares
        about people with disabilities.

Ableism and capitalism lock arms
Wrestling to see
    who can make people feel
        less worthy.
Less equipped to succeed based on inequality.
We don't ask for pity,
    we ask for accessibility.

It happened to me preemptively,
And I look "healthy,"
    which makes it harder
        for people to believe.
So I list off my series of disclosures,
Itemizing what damages have been incurred.
How much equity can be salvaged from
This house that has burned.

If only it was all in my head,
    like the doctors suggest.
Perhaps,
    the artist and patient
        share a common kismet.
Buried in debt.
Finally finding our success
    when we are dead.
A postmortem round of applause,
When the autopsy confirms
    all along
        what they repeatedly dismissed.
"She was in a world of pain,
    how could we have missed this?"

Texture

Be tan.
    Be skinny.
        Be voluptuous.
But most of all
    be flawless.
Have long straight hair,
But not just anywhere.
Your body,
    must be immaculately shaved,
        especially down there.

Emphasize the best bits,
    but shrink the rest.
Under-satiate your small waist,
    but feed your fat ass.
Enhance your breasts,
    but retain tiny thighs.
Like a commercially raised chicken,
    artificially enhanced.
Unable to stand,
From a lopsided body mass.
Falling over from skewed proportions,
    unnatural and grotesque.
We too,
    are engineered for our parts.
Pieced together to conform to their conditions of "beauty."
Our humanness,
Will never meet their definitions
    of how they think
        we should be.

History predicates that our wild female spaces be policed.
That our bodies are deemed okay to see,
    so long as we meet the conditions
Manicured by the mainstream.

At their behest,
We deflate our minds
    so as to not question the why.
Sinking in superficiality,
    drowning in lies.
Society can be mean,
But is ultimately meaningless.

I allowed myself to be misled
By conventional trends,
    believing their erroneous rumors.
So I tanned my skin,
Hoping to achieve their "ideal" amount of melanin.
I thought I would feel better about myself,
    but I was mistaken.
Once the bronze faded,
All that was left was tumors.

At thirty years old,
I have two burial plots,
One on my shoulder, the other my right hip.
Something buried in my tanned skin,
    a silent assassin.
Seven inches of flesh,
    dug out from moles,
        indistinguishable from melanoma.
The thing I did for beauty,
    nearly killed me.

Luckily,
I have embraced the Wabi Sabi of my fractures
        throughout the years.
Seeing my own unique elegance
        reflected in the cracks.
The beauty in deformity.

I began to buck the bad habit
Of misshaping myself
To fit into the fucked up shell
        of societal conformity.

They say beauty fades,
        but I disagree.
I think beauty grows in the fields of our freedoms.
In the naked faces
        and wild hair worn by loved ones
                that we adore.
In the delicate spots that we once ignored.
In the battlefield of mental health.
In the bravery,
        of showing up as yourself.
Beauty lives comfortably amongst the silhouette of wisdom.
Our aging eyes acting as prisms,
Reflecting the passage of time back at us.
We serve as our own hourglass.
Counting the value of our lives
        in the currency of memories,
This is the one true measure of wealth.

So burn the rules.
Allow wayward whiskered grass
        to grow up your knees.
The body is not a shrine,

It's a tethered vessel
        forged only to be lived in.
Housing grace within the fine lines
        of our texture.

The older I get
        the more I feel at home.
In the grain of my hair,
        course and untamed.
In my skin,
        speckled and raised.
I no longer seek airbrushed placidity,
Or shaved flattened lamination
        that strips us naked of complexity.
It doesn't feel rough enough,
Gritty enough,
        human enough to me.

In this life,
We plant trees along the way,
Each seeded with a different story.
Some, watered with laughter
        others swathed in sordid tragedy.
This forest of memories we cultivate is immortal.
One day,
When it's my time,
        and my imperfectly perfect body dies,
I will take my place below a canopy of Redwoods,
Falling into the malaise of an infinite daydream.
Cocooned by timbered rot,
My fingers will survey the underbrush,
Pleasured by the touch of glorious texture.
I promise,
The size of my thighs,
        will not be my last thought.

Toujours Chez Moi

"Always at home."
No matter where I wander,
Like a snail,
        I carry my home on my back.
Shelled safety is always a guarantee.
Protection is unassailable,
        so I travel freely
                allowing my nervous system to relax.

"Always at my place."
At this time and space,
Whenever,
        and wherever I show up,
I am precisely where I am meant to be.

Rejecting the assumption of early,
        or late.
Every action,
        every moment,
Has led to this intersection.

I am at ease and at peace
        in complete slowness.
Seeing that there's no need no rush or hustle,
When holding this knowing,
        there's a perfection to my pace.

GRATITUDE

•

To my mom, who gives me life again and again.
My husband, for being the buoy that keeps me afloat. The bee that pollinates dead flowers in the hope they bloom again.
My son, you are my reason. My sun, my guiding star in the darkness.

To Nana, Marilyn, a fellow poet. I see your rhymes reflected in the notes of the piano, in the words of poems written by your children and grandchildren. You say that those we love create our bliss, and that watching their wings take flight gives you renewed life. I will fly for you.

Polly, Amanda, and Jennifer without you, these words would live only in my mind. Thank you for your part in painting them on paper.

Caitlin, you taught me to listen to music by first knowing the people who created it. Only then, did I learn how to dance.

I am grateful for every person who has shared their story, despite the risk. May we each find refuge in this shared connection, allowing it to serve as a lighthouse; illuminating the way for the next generation of truth-tellers.

Regarding Restorative Justice: The survivor advocacy program is based out of Boulder, Colorado, championed by Greg and Denise. This method is controversial, but with you two at the helm it acts as a lifeline that restores the voice of survivors, returning choice, and opening an unexplored door to dialogue and healing. While my poem highlights a bad actor and a flawed system, this in no way represents what Greg and Denise have accomplished. They listened to me, believed me, and advocated for me in a way that I wish every survivor could experience. After the program, I was no longer afraid of my perpetrator, and indeed it was he who was too scared to face me.

ABOUT THE AUTHOR

Madisson Bednark is a poet from Denver, Colorado. After decades of living with trauma and combating several chronic illnesses, Madisson took two years to unravel the tangled threads of suffering and resilience, weaving them into the fabric of her debut publication and poetic memoir, *The Real Reason*. Driven by a deep passion for releasing pain, Madisson is on a mission to help other women heal. Outside of her artistic pursuits, she spends her time creating memories with her husband and son, crafting plant-based meals against the backdrop of Italian music, and doing handstands in strange places.

www.ingramcontent.com/pod-product-compliance
Lightning Source LLC
Chambersburg PA
CBHW022116090426
42743CB00008B/870